BRITISH HISTORY MAKERS

Edward the Confessor

Claire Throp

raintree

Raintree is an imprint of Capstone Global Library Limited, a company incorporated in England and Wales having its registered office at 264 Banbury Road, Oxford, OX2 7DY – Registered company number: 6695582

www.raintree.co.uk
myorders@raintree.co.uk

Edited by Linda Staniford
Designed by Steve Mead
Picture research by Ruth Smith
Production by Tori Abraham
Originated by Capstone Global Library

ISBN 978 1 474 73407 3 (hardback)
20 19 18 17 16
10 9 8 7 6 5 4 3 2 1

ISBN 978 1 474 73412 7 (paperback)
21 20 19 18 17
10 9 8 7 6 5 4 3 2 1

British Library Cataloguing in Publication Data
A full catalogue record for this book is available from the British Library

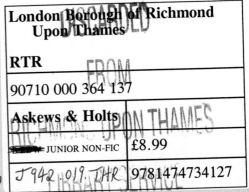

Acknowledgements
We would like to thank the following for permission to reproduce photographs:
Alamy: Chronicle, 16, Holmes Garden Photos, 15, Mary Evans Picture Library, 9, Michael Jenner; Bridgeman Images: English School, (20th century) / Private Collection/The Stapleton Collection, 4; Capstone Press: cover; Getty Images: Culture Club, 11, Historical Picture Archive/CORBIS, 24, Hulton Archive, 12; Glow Images: E&E Image Library, 5; Granger, NYC - All rights reserved: 13; iStockphoto: Duncan Walker, 10; Mary Evans Picture Library: cover; Newscom: akg-images / British Library, 14, Album/Florilegius, 20, CM Dixon Heritage Images, 26, The Print Collector Heritage Images, 21; Shutterstock: Aleks Melnik, cover, title page, Alfonso de Tomas, 8, Awe Inspiring Images, 6, Gala Matorina, cover, background design elements, Georgios Kollidas, 18, jorisvo, 25, Morphart Creation, 7, Toluk, cover, background design elements: Superstock: Peter Barritt, 17; Thinkstock: Photos. com, 19, 22, 23

We would like to thank Dr Mark Zumbuhl of the University of Oxford for his invaluable help in the preparation of this book.

Every effort has been made to contact copyright holders of material reproduced in this book. Any omissions will be rectified in subsequent printings if notice is given to the publisher.

All the Internet addresses (URLs) given in this book were valid at the time of going to press. However, due to the dynamic nature of the Internet, some addresses may have changed, or sites may have changed or ceased to exist since publication. While the author and publisher regret any inconvenience this may cause readers, no responsibility for any such changes can be accepted by either the author or the publisher.

Printed and bound in India

Some words are shown in bold, **like this**. You can find out what they mean by looking in the glossary.

Contents

Edward's life

Edward the Confessor is famous for being a very religious king. He was even made a **saint** many years after his death. But he did not make a clear choice about who would become king when he died. This resulted in the **Normans invading** Britain in 1066.

⊙ FACT ⊙

Edward ordered the first Westminster Abbey to be built in London in the 1040s.

History

From AD 787, people known as the Vikings **invaded** Britain. They came from Norway, Denmark and Sweden. By the middle of the 800s, the Vikings were settling in some parts of Britain. In 886, King Alfred the Great stopped them from taking over the whole country. They agreed that some areas would be ruled by **Anglo-Saxons** and some by the Vikings.

∽ FACT ∽

Alfred's agreement with the Vikings was called the Danelaw. A Dane is someone who comes from Denmark.

Early life

Edward was born in Islip, Oxfordshire, between 1002 and 1005. His parents were Ethelred II (the Unready) and his wife, Emma of Normandy. The Vikings invaded Britain again in 1013, forcing Edward's family to move to Normandy in France. They returned to England in 1014 when Ethelred was able to rule once more. But after Ethelred died in 1016, Edward went back to Normandy.

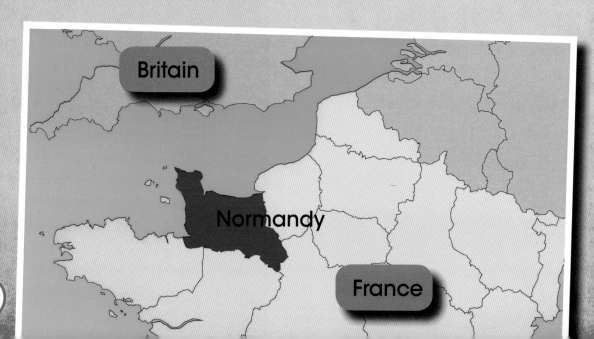

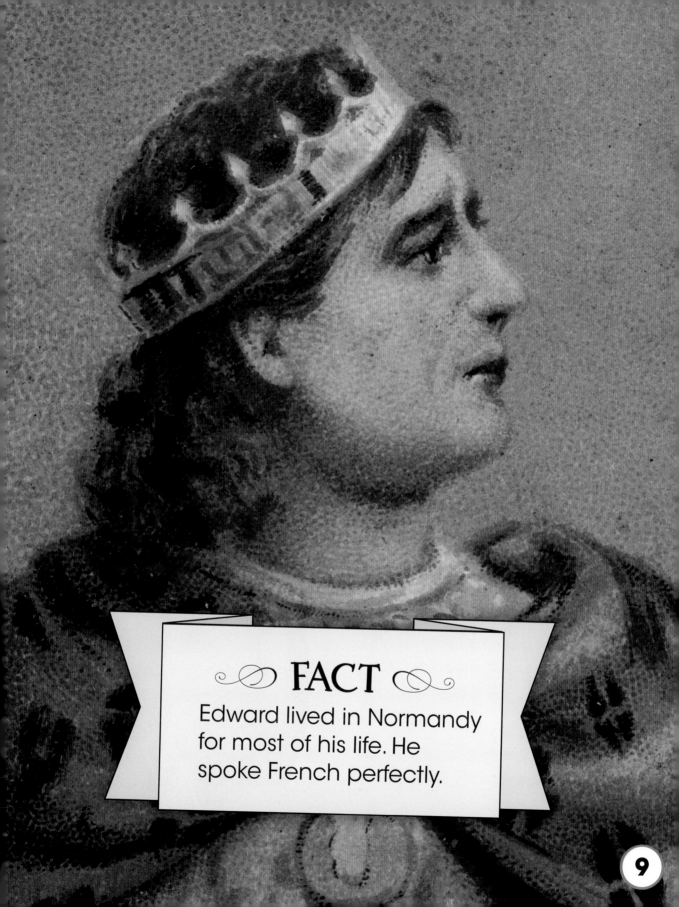

FACT

Edward lived in Normandy for most of his life. He spoke French perfectly.

Harthacnut

After Ethelred died, Edward's mother, Emma, married King Cnut. They had a son called Harthacnut. He became king after Cnut's death. Harthacnut had no children. So he asked his half-brother Edward to return to England as **heir** to the throne. Harthacnut died in June 1042.

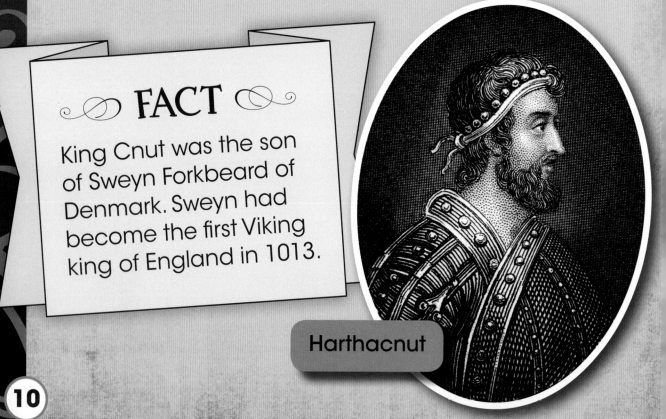

⟬ FACT ⟭

King Cnut was the son of Sweyn Forkbeard of Denmark. Sweyn had become the first Viking king of England in 1013.

Harthacnut

Cnut and Emma

11

King Edward

In 1042, Edward was crowned king. Godwine, Earl of Wessex, was one of the most powerful men in England. He helped to get Edward on the throne. He thought he'd be able to control Edward.

⊷ FACT ⊷

When Edward was crowned, he was given a sapphire ring. The sapphire jewel is now in the Imperial State Crown. The crown is worn by the Queen on important occasions.

Godwine and Edward

Godwine was the real ruler of England for the first 11 years of Edward's **reign**. He owned nearly as much land as the king. He became even more powerful after Edward married Edith, Godwine's daughter, in 1045.

This is a page from the *Anglo-Saxon Chronicle*.

15

Edward's French brother-in-law, Eustace of Boulogne, visited England in 1051. A fight broke out between Eustace's men and some local Anglo-Saxons in Dover, part of Godwine's land. Edward asked Godwine to punish those involved, but Godwine refused. With support from the powerful earls of Northumberland and Mercia, Edward forced Godwine to leave England.

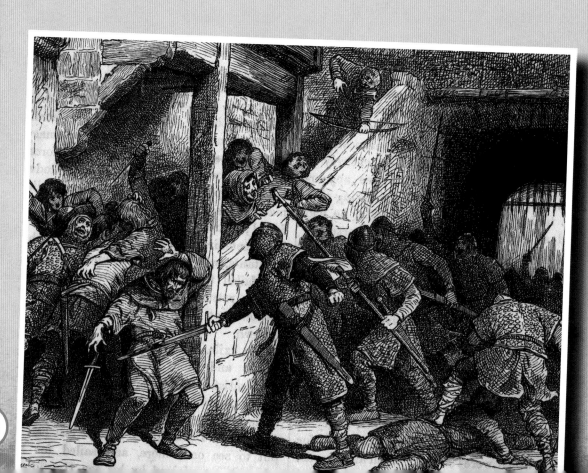

Norman power

During 1051, Edward gave many of his Norman friends important positions at court. Edward's cousin William of Normandy visited at this time. Edward may have offered to make William his heir. The Anglo-Saxon **nobles** who had supported Edward against Godwine were unhappy. They did not like the thought of the Normans taking power.

William of Normandy

FACT

The Anglo-Saxon nobles who helped the king to rule were called the Witan.

Godwine's return

Godwine raised an army against Edward in 1052. He attacked the Isle of Wight and then sailed up the coast and on to London. Edward had sent men to fight Godwine, but they refused. Nobody wanted to support the king. Edward was forced to accept Godwine's return. Many Normans escaped or were sent away from court.

Godwine's army sailed in ships like these.

Edward did not have many supporters left.

⌐∾ FACT ∾⌐

The earls of Mercia and Northumberland had been on Edward's side against Godwine. In the end they joined Godwine!

Harold Godwineson

Godwine died in 1053. His son Harold became Earl of Wessex. He got on well with Edward. By 1063, the English and Welsh had been fighting for some years. Harold led an English army to defeat the Welsh. He also defeated the Northumbrians two years later.

The Bayeux Tapestry shows the events leading up to the Battle of Hastings. This section shows Edward on his throne.

∞ FACT ∞

In 1064, Harold went to France. He was captured by some of William of Normandy's men. The Normans claimed that Harold promised to support William's right to be king after Edward's death.

Edward's death

In November 1065, Edward became ill. He had no children, so it is thought that he named Harold as his heir. Edward died on 5 January 1066. Harold was crowned king the next day. William of Normandy was furious. He claimed that he was Edward's heir. William invaded England.

FACT

King Harold was killed at the Battle of Hastings in October 1066. William became king.

Legacy

Edward's reign was mostly peaceful. But he did not make it clear who was to be king after his death. This led to the end of the Anglo-Saxon kings.

In the 1130s, a **monk** called Osbert of Clare wrote about Edward's life. He claimed that **miracles** had taken place at Edward's **tomb**. In 1161, Edward was made a saint.

Timeline

1002 or 1005 Edward born in Islip, Oxfordshire, to King Ethelred II and Emma of Normandy

1013 Sweyn becomes England's first Viking king after defeating Ethelred; Edward and his family move to Normandy, France

1041 Edward comes to Harthacnut's court in England

1042 Harthacnut dies in June

1042 Edward becomes King of England with the support of Godwine of Wessex

1045 Edward marries Edith, Godwine's daughter

1051 Edward forces Godwine out of England after Godwine refuses to punish people involved in a riot at Dover

1052 Godwine and his sons raise an army against Edward; Edward is forced to return Godwine's land and title

1053 Godwine dies and his son Harold becomes the new Earl of Wessex

1066 Edward the Confessor dies on 5 January after supposedly naming Harold as his heir

1066 Harold crowned on 6 January

1066 William of Normandy successfully invades England and becomes king

1161 Edward the Confessor is made a saint

Glossary

Anglo-Saxons people who lived in England from the AD 400s

heir person who is next in line to rule a country

invade send an army into a country in order to take over the country

miracle something that cannot be explained easily

monk man who lives in a religious community and promises to devote his life to his religion

noble wealthy person of high rank or birth

Normans people from Normandy in France

reign time during which a king or queen rules over their country

saint person who Christians think is very holy and good

tomb place where a body is buried

Find out more

Books
Anglo-Saxons (Fact Cat), Izzi Howell (Wayland, 2016)
Everyday Life (Discover the Anglo-Saxons), Moira Butterfield
    (Franklin Watts, 2016)
The Battle of Hastings (Why Do We Remember?), Claudia Martin
    (Franklin Watts, 2016)

Websites
anglosaxondiscovery.ashmolean.org
Learn more about the Anglo-Saxon way of life.

www.bbc.co.uk/schools/primaryhistory/anglo_saxons
Find out about the Anglo-Saxons on this website.

www.bbc.co.uk/schools/primaryhistory/vikings
This website has lots of information about the Vikings.

Place to visit
Westminster Abbey
20 Deans Yard, Westminster, London SW1P 3PA
Visit the shrine at Westminster Abbey to see the tomb of Edward
the Confessor.

Index